SADIE: THE DOG
WHO FINDS THE EVIDENCE

BY THEA FELDMAN ★ ILLUSTRATED BY CHRIS DANGER

Ready-to-Read

Simon Spotlight

New York　　London　　Toronto　　Sydney　　New Delhi

SIMON SPOTLIGHT
An imprint of Simon & Schuster Children's Publishing Division
1230 Avenue of the Americas, New York, New York 10020
© 2014 American Humane Association. The American Humane Association Hero Dog Awards™ is a trademark
of American Humane Association.
SIMON SPOTLIGHT, READY-TO-READ, and colophon are registered trademarks of Simon & Schuster, Inc.
For information about special discounts for bulk purchases, please contact Simon & Schuster Special Sales at
1-866-506-1949 or business@simonandschuster.com.
The Simon & Schuster Speakers Bureau can bring authors to your live event. For more information or to book
an event contact the Simon & Schuster Speakers Bureau at 1-866-248-3049 or visit our website at
www.simonspeakers.com.
Manufactured in the United States of America 0814 LAK
First Edition
Library of Congress Cataloging-in-Publication Data
Feldman, Thea.
Sadie : the dog who finds the evidence / Thea Feldman ; illustrated by Chris Danger.
pages cm. — (Hero dog)
Summary: "Meet Sadie, a real dog who works with the Colorado Bureau of Investigation, in this inspiring,
Level 2 Ready-to-Read based on one of the winners of the annual American Humane Association's Hero Dog
Awards™! Meet Sadie. Sadie has an important job as an Arson Dog with the Colorado Bureau of Investigation.
Because her sense of smell is 100 times stronger than a human's, she helps firefighters and police officers
find the causes of fires. That makes her a hero to many people. When she's not busy sniffing out the bad guys,
Sadie visits schools to teach kids about fire safety! Read her action-packed story to find out more about what
this amazing canine does and what makes Sadie a hero! Emerging readers will love discovering the inspiring,
action-packed story of a different heroic dog in each book of the Hero Dog series. ©2014 American Humane
Association. The American Humane Association Hero Dog Awards™ is a trademark of the American Humane
Association"— Provided by publisher.
ISBN 978-1-4814-2240-6 (paperback) — ISBN 978-1-4814-2241-3 (hardcover) — ISBN 978-1-4814-2242-0 (eBook)
1. Service dogs—Juvenile literature. I. Danger, Chris, illustrator. II. Title.
HV1569.6.F45 2014
363.25'96420929—dc23
2014003801

"Seek, Sadie. Seek!"

Jerry tells his dog, Sadie.

Sadie knows just what to do.

Sadie leads the way into the house.
Jerry holds on to her leash
and follows her inside.
The house has been in a fire.
Everything has been destroyed.

Most dogs would not want to go
inside a house that has burned.
It smells from the fire,
and it can be dangerous.
But Sadie does not hesitate.

Sadie is an arson dog.
She has investigated
hundreds of fires.
Jerry is her partner
and her best friend.
They work together for the
Colorado Bureau of Investigation.
They investigate the causes of fires.

Some people start fires on purpose.
It can be hard to catch them
after everything has burned.
But not with Sadie on the job!

Sadie can smell and find even the tiniest amount of fuel or other things that can be used to start a fire. Sadie's sense of smell is 100 times stronger than a human's.

Her nose can find things that people can't, and it can find things faster than machines.

Sadie and her nose are the best equipment that a fire investigator like Jerry can have!

Inside the house, Sadie walks past
many things that have burned.
She steps over loose boards
that have sharp nails sticking up.

She walks around a big hole
in the floor.

Sadie wags her tail.
She keeps her head low.
She sniffs everything she passes.

After just a few minutes,
Sadie sits down.

Sadie points to a pile of burnt wood
with her long nose.
She bobs her head up and down.
She is telling Jerry,
"I found something! Look over here!"

"Good job, Sadie!" says Jerry.
He pats her on her head.
Then he gives Sadie some food.
It is her reward.

Investigators take samples from
the spot Sadie found.
They test them and find gasoline.
That means someone did
set fire to the house on purpose.

The police are able to find
and arrest the person
who started the fire.
That person will not start another
fire that could destroy more
property or hurt other people!
It's all thanks to Sadie
and her well-trained nose.

Sadie is a hero!
But Sadie is just doing her job.
It is a job she loves.

When Jerry puts Sadie in her vest, she is always ready to go to work.

Sadie was not always an arson dog.
One day Sadie was adopted.
She was paired with Jerry.
The two have been together
every day since then.

Sadie was chosen by the
State Farm Arson Dog Program
to attend dog school in Maine
and learn how to be an arson dog.
Sadie learned to recognize the odors
of more than sixty different things
that can start a fire.

Sadie and Jerry work together
all 365 days of the year.
Every day they practice
what they learned in school.
Sadie has not had a day off
in many years!

Jerry hides a tiny amount
of something that can start a fire.
Sadie does not see where he hid it,
but she always finds it!

One day, Sadie was working
at the scene of a fire.
She sniffed the shoes of people
in the crowd that had gathered.

She sniffed something on
the shoes of two people.
Not much later, they confessed
to starting the fire!

On some days Jerry and Sadie
go to schools to teach kids
about fire safety.

Sadie gets a lot of applause
and a lot of hugs.

Jerry is very proud of Sadie.
She does important work
that can be dangerous.
She saves lives!
She goes anywhere she is needed,
at any time.
And she always seems happy.

Jerry thought there should be a statue that honors arson dogs. Today there is a National Fire Dog Monument in Washington, D.C. Sadie was the model for the dog in the statue!

And that's not all!
One year, Sadie was honored
as the most courageous dog
of her kind
at the American Humane Association
Hero Dog Awards!